WORLD WAR TWO PLANES
COLOURING BOOK

Published by IWM, Lambeth Road, London SE1 6HZ
iwm.org.uk

ISBN 978-1-912423-55-2

A catalogue record for this book is available
from the British Library.

Printed and bound by Gomer Press Limited
Illustrations by Frances Castle

Every effort has been made to contact all copyright holders.
The publishers will be glad to make good in future editions
any error or omissions brought to their attention.

WORLD WAR TWO PLANES COLOURING BOOK

Illustrations by
Frances Castle

*A **SUPERMARINE SPITFIRE** PREPARES FOR TAKE-OFF DURING THE BATTLE OF FRANCE, 1940.*

THREE **BRISTOL BLENHEIMS**
IN FORMATION.

AN AIR BATTLE BETWEEN A **HAWKER HURRICANE** AND A **'STUKA'** **JUNKERS JU 87**.

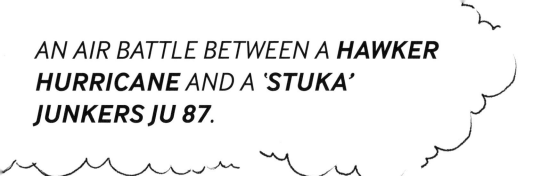

PREVIOUS PAGE... A DOGFIGHT BETWEEN A **SUPERMARINE SPITFIRE** AND A **MESSERSCHMITT BF 109** DURING THE BATTLE OF BRITAIN, 1940.

HEINKEL HE 111S FLYING OVER LONDON DURING THE BLITZ, SEPTEMBER 1940.

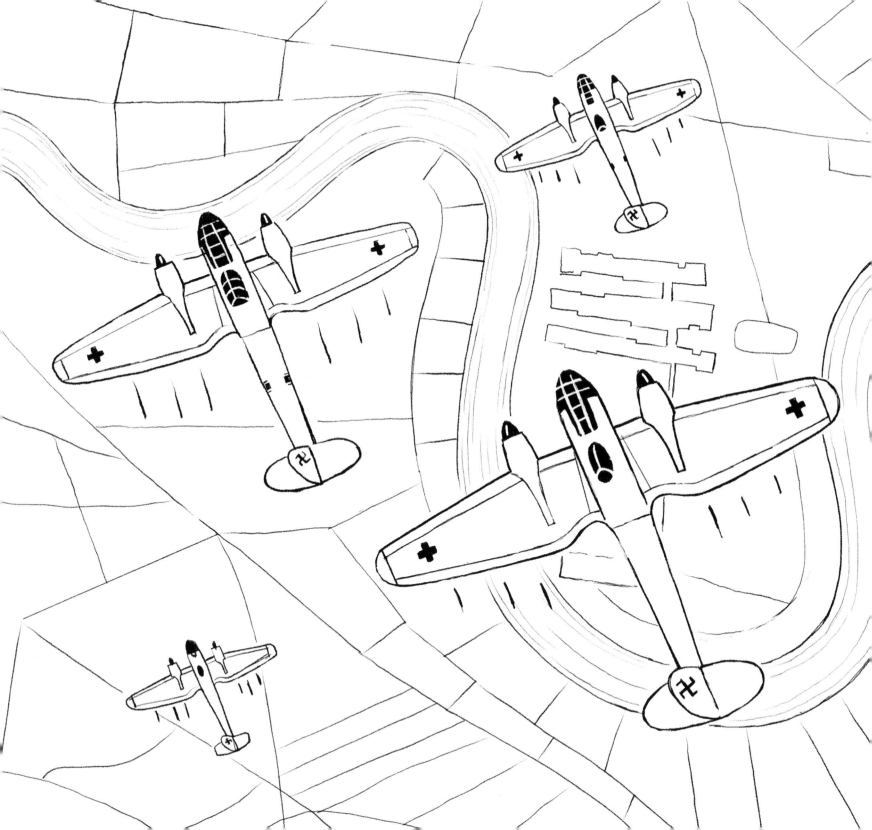

A **BELL P-39 AIRACOBRA** IN OPERATION WITH A **LOCKHEED P-38 LIGHTNING** AND A **CURTISS P-40 WARHAWK**.

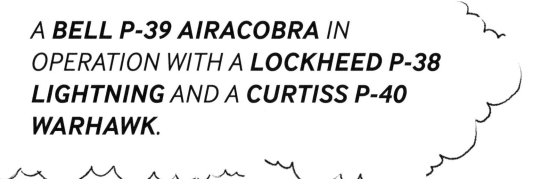

THE ITALIAN FLEET AT ANCHOR UNDER ATTACK FROM **FAIREY SWORDFISH** AT THE BATTLE OF TARANTO, NOVEMBER 1940.

THREE VICKERS WELLINGTONS *DROPPING BOMBS OVER ENEMY TERRITORY.*

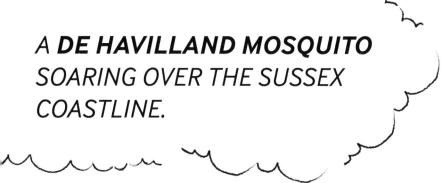

A **DE HAVILLAND MOSQUITO** SOARING OVER THE SUSSEX COASTLINE.

*A **YAKOVLEV YAK-1** IN BATTLE WITH A **MESSERSCHMITT BF 109** DURING OPERATION BARBAROSSA, 1941.*

*A **CURTISS P-36 HAWK** GOES TOE-TO-TOE WITH A **MITSUBISHI A6M2 ZERO** OVER PEARL HARBOR, DECEMBER 1941.*

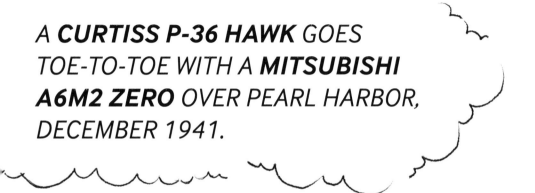

*A SQUADRON OF **SHORT STIRLINGS** SETTING OFF ON A RAID OVER ENEMY TERRITORY.*

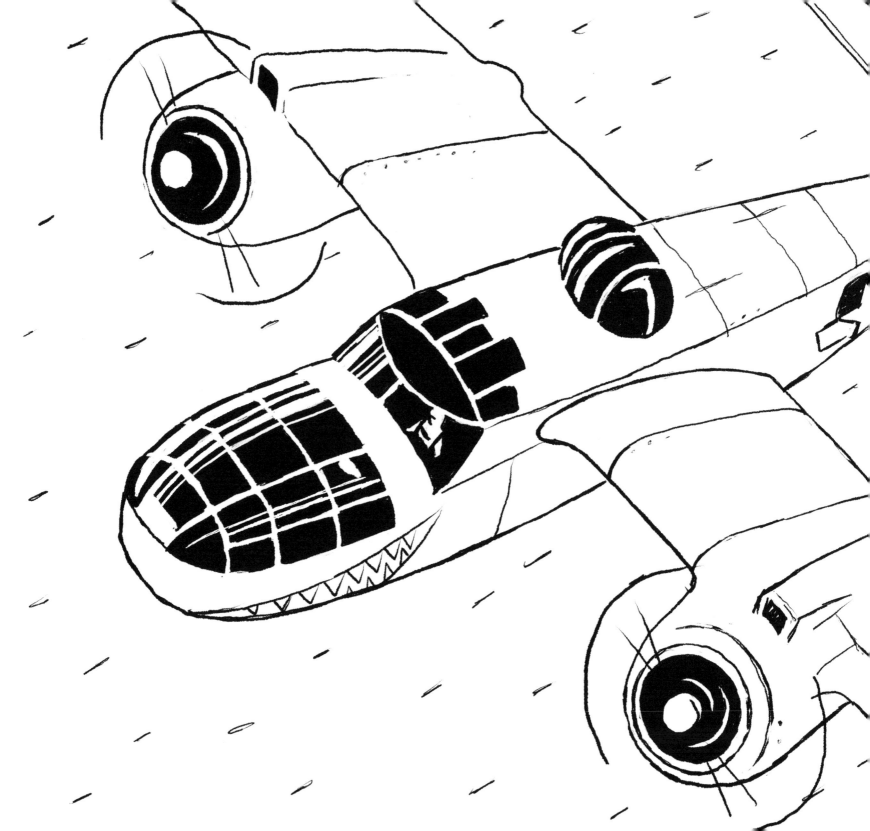

PREVIOUS PAGE... **NORTH AMERICAN B-25 MITCHELLS** *TAKING OFF FROM AN AIRCRAFT CARRIER DURING THE DOOLITTLE RAID, 18 APRIL 1942.*

*TWO **AVRO LANCASTER BOMBERS** IN ACTION OVER A GERMAN CITY.*

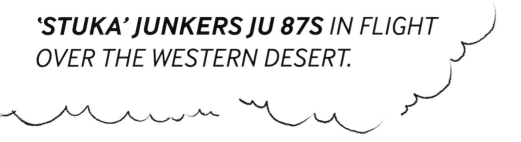

'STUKA' JUNKERS JU 87S IN FLIGHT
OVER THE WESTERN DESERT.

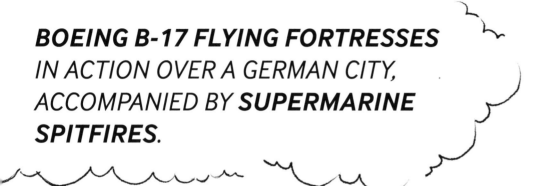

BOEING B-17 FLYING FORTRESSES IN ACTION OVER A GERMAN CITY, ACCOMPANIED BY **SUPERMARINE SPITFIRES**.

'FLASH', A GERMAN SHEPHERD DOG AND MASCOT OF RAF DUXFORD'S NO. 19 SQUADRON, SITTING ON THE NOSE OF A **SPITFIRE**.

A **CONSOLIDATED PBY CATALINA LANDING** NEXT TO A FLEET OF US NAVY AIRCRAFT CARRIERS.

GROUND CREW SERVICING A
REPUBLIC P-47 THUNDERBOLT.

A **BOEING B-17 FLYING FORTRESS**
AND **P-51 MUSTANG** IN FORMATION.

A **CONSOLIDATED B-24 LIBERATOR**
SWOOPING OVER NAPLES, ITALY.

*PREVIOUS PAGE... **AVRO LANCASTERS** DROPPING BOUNCING BOMBS ON A GERMAN DAM DURING THE DAMBUSTERS RAID, MAY 1943.*

*A **SHORT SUNDERLAND** TRACKING A SURFACING U-BOAT.*

PLOTTERS AT WORK IN THE 'NERVE CENTRE' OF AN RAF STATION. THEY RECEIVE INFORMATION ON THE POSITION OF FRIENDLY AND ENEMY AIRCRAFT AND PLOT THEIR COURSES ON THE TABLE MAPS FOR RAF CONTROLLERS.

*A **MESSERSCHMITT ME 262** SOARING THROUGH THE SKY.*

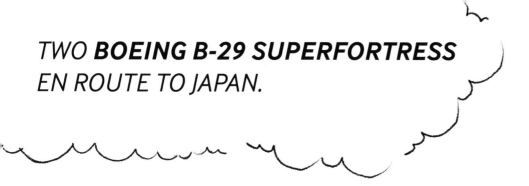

TWO **BOEING B-29 SUPERFORTRESS**
EN ROUTE TO JAPAN.

*A **VOUGHT F4U CORSAIR** FLYING OVER THE JUNGLES OF GUAM.*

A **WESTLAND LYSANDER**
LANDING AT NIGHT IN FRANCE.

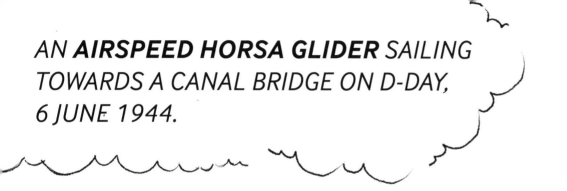

AN **AIRSPEED HORSA GLIDER** SAILING
TOWARDS A CANAL BRIDGE ON D-DAY,
6 JUNE 1944.

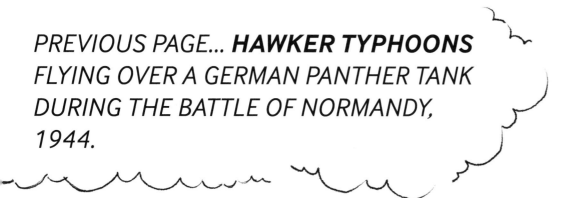

PREVIOUS PAGE... **HAWKER TYPHOONS** FLYING OVER A GERMAN PANTHER TANK DURING THE BATTLE OF NORMANDY, 1944.

PARATROOPERS DROPPING FROM **DOUGLAS C-47 SKYTRAINS** OVER THE OUTSKIRTS OF ARNHEM, NETHERLANDS, DURING OPERATION MARKET GARDEN, 17 SEPTEMBER 1944.

*A **DE HAVILLAND VAMPIRE** FLYING OVER SNOW-COVERED MOUNTAINS.*

SPITFIRE PM655 BANKING
AWAY WHILE IN FLIGHT.

*A **YOKOSUKA MXY-7 OHKA** IS RELEASED FROM A **MITSUBISHI G4M 'BETTY' BOMBER**, READYING FOR A KAMIKAZE ATTACK.*

The aircraft featured in this colouring book are just a snippet of the many that participated in World War Two. Inspired by photographs and artworks from IWM's collections, the illustrations within these pages offer artistic interpretations of key scenes from the air battles over Europe and beyond.